First World War
and Army of Occupation
War Diary
France, Belgium and Germany

57 DIVISION
170 Infantry Brigade
Loyal North Lancashire Regiment
2/5th Battalion (Territorial Force)
8 February 1917 - 30 January 1918

WO95/2979/3

The Naval & Military Press Ltd
www.nmarchive.com
Published in association with The National Archives

Published by

The Naval & Military Press Ltd

Unit 10 Ridgewood Industrial Park,
Uckfield, East Sussex,
TN22 5QE England
Tel: +44 (0) 1825 749494

www.naval-military-press.com

www.nmarchive.com

This diary has been reprinted in facsimile from the original. Any imperfections are inevitably reproduced and the quality may fall short of modern type and cartographic standards.

© Crown Copyright
Images reproduced by permission of The National Archives, London, England, 2015.

Contents

Document type	Place/Title	Date From	Date To
Heading	WO95/2979-3		
Heading	War Diary Of 2/5th Loyal North Lancashire Regiment From 8/2/17 To 28/2/17 Volume 1		
War Diary	Blackdown	08/02/1917	08/02/1917
War Diary	Outtersteene	12/02/1917	18/02/1917
War Diary	Fleurbaix Sector	22/02/1917	28/02/1917
Heading	War Diary Of 2/5 Loyal North Lancashire Regt From March 1st /17 To March 31st/17 Volume No.2		
War Diary	Fleurbaix Sector	02/03/1917	27/03/1917
War Diary	Cordonnerie Sector	02/03/1917	27/03/1917
Heading	War Diary Of 2/5 Loyal North Lancs Regt From April 1st/17 To April 30th/17 Volume 3		
War Diary	Cordonnerie Sector	01/04/1917	30/04/1917
Heading	War Diary Of 2/5 Loyal North Lancashire Regt From May 1st /1917 To May 31st 1917 Volume No.4		
War Diary	Cordonnerie Sector	01/05/1917	28/05/1917
War Diary	Dac St. Maur	31/05/1917	31/05/1917
Heading	War Diary Of 2/5 Loyal North Lancashire Regt From June 1st/1917 To June 30th/1917 Volume 5		
War Diary	Bac St Maur	01/06/1917	02/06/1917
War Diary	Ploegsteert Wood	03/06/1917	11/06/1917
War Diary	Armentieres	11/06/1917	11/06/1917
War Diary	Bac St Maur	12/06/1917	14/06/1917
War Diary	Cordonnerie Sector	19/06/1917	30/06/1917
Heading	War Diary Of 2/5 Loyal North Lancashire Regt From July 1st/1917 To July 31st 1917 Volume 6		
War Diary	Cordonnerie Sector	01/07/1917	31/07/1917
Heading	War Diary Of 2/5 Loyal North Lancashire Regt From August 1st 1917 To August 31st 1917		
War Diary	Armentieres	01/08/1917	01/08/1917
War Diary	L'Epinette Sector	01/08/1917	31/08/1917
Heading	War Diary Of 2/5 Batt Loyal North Lancashire Regt From Sept 1st 1917 To Sept 30th 1917		
War Diary	Armentieres	01/09/1917	19/09/1917
War Diary	Cantrainne	20/09/1917	30/09/1917
Heading	War Diary Of 2/5 Bn Loyal North Lancashire Regt From October 1st 1917 To October 31st 1917		
War Diary	Westrehem	01/10/1917	17/10/1917
War Diary	Renescure	18/10/1917	18/10/1917
War Diary	Boesinghe Marsouin Fm	23/10/1917	23/10/1917
War Diary	Line N.E. Of Poelcappelle	24/10/1917	31/10/1917
Heading	War Diary Of 2/5 Battalion Loyal North Lancs Regt From November 1st 1917 To November 30th 1917		
War Diary	Proven Area No.1	01/11/1917	02/11/1917
War Diary	Piddington Camp	03/11/1917	08/11/1917
War Diary	Audenfort	10/11/1917	30/11/1917
Heading	War Diary Of 2/5 Bn Loyal North Lancs. Regt From Dec 1st 1917 To Dec 31st 1917		
War Diary	Audenfort	01/12/1917	31/12/1917
War Diary	Portsmouth Camp	01/01/1918	01/01/1918

War Diary	Proven	02/01/1918	02/01/1918
War Diary	Wez Macquart Sector	03/01/1918	30/01/1918
Heading	57th Division 170th Infy Bde 4-5th Bn Loy. Nth Lancs 1915 Oct 1916 Feb 1917 Feb 1918 Jan		

(2979) 15/9 om

(2979) 25/9 om

Vol I 17º/5¹

CONFIDENTIAL.

WAR DIARY

of

2/5th Loyal North Lancashire Regiment.

From 8/2/17. To 28/2/17.

Volume 1.

Army Form C. 2118

WAR DIARY
or
INTELLIGENCE SUMMARY
(Erase heading not required.)

Instructions regarding War Diaries and Intelligence Summaries are contained in F.S. Regs., Part II. and the Staff Manual respectively. Title Pages will be prepared in manuscript.

Place	Date	Hour	Summary of Events and Information	Remarks and references to Appendices
BLACKDOWN	8/2/17	5.0 am	The Battalion left Blackdown for France. Strength 37 Off. 989 O. Ranks	Ctd
OUTTERSTEENE	17/2/17	11.0 am	The Battalion established in Billets in the outskirts of Outtersteene in preparation to taking over a portion of the line.	Ctd
	18/2/17	9.0 am	The Battalion moved by road and relieved the 2nd Batt 3rd N.Z.(R) Bde. who were in Divisional reserve, Billets.	Ctd
FLEURBAIX SECTOR	20/2/17	10.0 am	The Battalion commenced relieving the 1/5 Kings own Royal Lancs. Regt. Coy by Coy. relief completed Sunday 25/2/17. 11.30 am. Sector taken over. (Ref map. 36. N.W.) N9d. 7b. 55. to N4.d. 85.00.	Ctd
	26/2/17	12.30 pm	5 O.Ranks killed in action. 30 Ranks Wounded	
	27/2/17		1 Wounded. (Shell shock.)	
	28/2/17		1 Officer (2nd Lieut. H.L. BANGHAM 1/7th Welch Regt. att 1/5 L.N. Lancs.) wounded	Ctd

57

CONFIDENTIAL. Vol 2

WAR DIARY.
of
2/5 LOYAL NORTH LANCASHIRE REGT.

from March 1st/17 to March 31st/17.

VOLUME No. 2.

WAR DIARY
or
INTELLIGENCE SUMMARY

Army Form C. 2118

(Erase heading not required.)

Place	Date	Hour	Summary of Events and Information	Remarks and references to Appendices
FLEURBAIX SECTOR	2nd	8.0pm	Battalion relieved by 7/5 Kings Own R/Lanc Regt. & concerned tasks over district in Brigade Reserve.	
	8th	9.15am	'C' Coy + 1 Plat 'B' Coy proceeded to Divisional Raid School for instructional purposes (returned on the 17th inst.)	
	9th	7.0am	'D' Coy + 1 Plat 'B' Coy relieved 7th L.N.Lancs Regt and took over the whole of the Brigade Subsidiary Line.	
	11th	6.0pm	the Battalion relieved the 7th Royal York Lancs Regt. and took over the RIGHT of the Brigade Sector.	
	12th	1.0am	3 men gassed.	
	19th	9.50am	The Battalion was relieved by 7th L.N.Lancs Regt & took over Brigade Reserve.	
	27th	8.0pm	the Battalion relieved the 7th L.N.Lancs in the line.	

WAR DIARY or INTELLIGENCE SUMMARY

Army Form C. 2118

Month: March 1917

Place	Date	Hour	Summary of Events and Information	Remarks and references to Appendices
	2nd	8.0pm	Battalion relieved by 2/5 Kings Own R. Lancs Regt. & proceeded to take over billets in Brigade Reserve.	
	8th	9.15am	'C' Coy + 1 Plat. 'B' Coy proceeded to Divisional Raid School (returned on the 14th inst.)	
	9th	7am	'D' Coy + 1 Plat. 'B' Coy relieved 7th L.N. Lancs Regt and took over the whole of the Brigade Subsidiary Line.	
	11th	6pm	The Battalion relieved the 7th Loyal North Lancs Regt. and took over the Right Brigade Sector.	
	12th	10am	3 men gassed. (see other)	
	19th	9.30	The Battalion was relieved by 7th L.N. Lancs Regt & took over Brigade Reserve.	
	27th	8.0pm	The Battalion relieved the 7th L.Lancs in the Line	

CORDONNERIE SECTOR.

55/57

Vol 3

CONFIDENTIAL.

WAR DIARY

OF

2/5 LOYAL NORTH LANCS. REGT.

From April 1st/17 to April 30th/17

VOLUME. 3.

Army Form C. 2118

WAR DIARY
or
INTELLIGENCE SUMMARY
(Erase heading not required.)

April/1917

Place	Date	Hour	Summary of Events and Information	Remarks and references to Appendices
CROONAERE SECTOR	1/4/17	12 mid	Strength 34 off. 950 o ranks.	
	3/4/17	10.25 pm	The Battalion was relieved by the 7th Royal North Lancs Regt.	
do	12/4/17	12 mid	The Battalion relieved the Loyal North Lancs Regt.	
	13/4/17	7 am	1 Officer wounded. LIEUT. E.W. MEAD O.T.S.	
	16/4/17	12.30 pm	1 Officer killed. MAJOR W. AINSWORTH 2nd in Command.	
do	19/4/17	8.0 pm (mid.)	The Battalion was relieved by the 4th Loyal N. Lancs Regt. & took over Bde Reserve. During the term Enemy machine gun active. 2 enemy patrols approached our front line but were driven back, on one occasion left 2 dead, no identifications were discovered.	
do	27/4/17	12 mid	The Battalion relieved the Loyal N. Lancs.	
	30/4/17	12 mid	Strength 35 off. 892 o ranks.	O'Rourke

CONFIDENTIAL.

WAR DIARY
of
2/5 LOYAL NORTH LANCASHIRE REGT.

From May 1st/1917. To May 31st 1917.

Volume No 4.

Vol 4

WAR DIARY or INTELLIGENCE SUMMARY

Army Form C. 2118

May 1917

Place	Date	Hour	Summary of Events and Information	Remarks and references to Appendices
CORDONNERIE SECTOR	1/5/17	9.30am	Strength of Battalion 35 Officers 892 O'Ranks	
	5/5/17	11.30pm	The Battalion was Relieved by 1st K.R.Rifles Regt. (10th over the Reserve. Nothing unusual, Artillery normal.	
	9/5/17	11.25pm	The Battalion Relieved 7th Lufano Regt. in the line.	
	13/5/17	11.45pm	The Battalion was Relieved by the Royal Hanover & took over the Reserve. Nothing unusual. Artillery normal.	
	18/5/17	11.30pm	The Battalion Relieved the 7th Lufano Regt. in the line.	
	19/5/17	11.0pm	The Battalion carried out a <u>Silent Raid</u>. Strength of Raiding Party 3 Off. 3rd O'Ranks. Enemy had apparently cleared his front & support line preparatory to a Trench Mortar Shoot which commenced shortly after. Raiders left our line, no enemy were encountered, the Raiders stayed in Boche lines 4 hour. No prisoners. Casualties Nil. Zero hour was at 11.0pm.	
	27/5/17	10.0pm	The Battalion carried out a Silent Raid. Strength 2 Off. 15 O'Ranks. Before the Raiders had arrived at enemy outpost line a Boche patrol was heard. Raiders split into 2 parties "A" Party "B" Party. "A" Party surprised them. Finally "B" Party rushed the Boche patrol with Bayonets, a fight ensued ending	

WAR DIARY
or
INTELLIGENCE SUMMARY

May 1917 (Cnt'd)

Army Form C. 2118

Place	Date	Hour	Summary of Events and Information	Remarks and references to Appendices
CORDONNERIE SECTOR	24/5/17	10.0 pm	Ending in 4 Enemy being captured & tonight Pack. 2 O/R's Broke Patrol were killed. Our Casualties :- 1. Off Wounded :- Lt P. CRAMPTON. 2 of the Enemy prisoners were Jon Caro Richards, all four sturdy & in very good physical condition.	
	28/5/17	12.32 am	A very successful Raid was the outcome of careful reconnaissance. The Battalion was relieved by 1/4 West Riding Regt. & proceeded to BKS. ST MAUR & Billets.	
BKS. ST MAUR.	31/5/17	12 m	Strength 34 Officers. 888 O'ranks	

E. Wark
Capt & adj
1/5 Manch Regt

Vol. 5

CONFIDENTIAL

WAR DIARY:

OF

2/5 LOYAL NORTH LANCASHIRE REGT

From June 1st/1917 To June 30th/1917.

Volume. 5.

Army Form C. 2118

WAR DIARY
or
INTELLIGENCE SUMMARY
(Erase heading not required.)

June 1/17

Place	Date	Hour	Summary of Events and Information	Remarks and references to Appendices
BAC ST MAUR.	1/6/17	8.0 a.m	The Battalion marched to ARMENTIÈRES & billeted for the night. Strength 34 - 886 ranks.	
	2/6/17		The Battalion marched to the trenches via PLOEGSTEERT Wood o-o-o the LEFT Subsector of the LE TOUQUET SECTOR (PLOEGSTEERT WOOD) Relieving the 42nd Bn. A.I.F. Relief Complete 12 mid. On this date the Battalion along with the 16 Royal Munster Regt. became detached from the 70 Inf. Bde, & was formed into the 57th Div. Detached force under command of Lt. Col. Lenan D.S.O. This detached force being under the command of the 3rd Australian Division. The detached force was formed and attached to the 3rd Australian Division for the purpose of holding the pivot or Right Flank of the 2nd ARMY attack on MESSINES RIDGE. Frontage of Battalion WARNAVE RIVER (U28C 20,80.) to WESTMINSTER Av. took place. Relief in this date was carried out quickly & without casualties under heavy enemy shell fire.	Q CN

WAR DIARY
or
INTELLIGENCE SUMMARY

Army Form C. 2118

(Erase heading not required.)

June 1917

Place	Date	Hour	Summary of Events and Information	Remarks and references to Appendices
POELSTRAAT WOOD	3/6/17	12 noon	Enemy & Own Artillery very active on whole sector. Casualties: O.Ranks. 3 wounded.	
"	4/6/17	12 noon	Artillery on both sides very active. Casualties O.Ranks. 3 killed 3 wounded.	
	5/6/17	noon	Artillery on both sides very active. Enemy shelled whole sector heavily during the whole previous 24 hours. Casualties: O.Ranks. 2 killed 9 wounded.	
	6/6/17	noon	Artillery in charge & heavy shelling by both sides. Casualties O.Ranks 21 wounded.	
	8/6/17 to 7/6/17	10.35 pm 2.30 am	Enemy shelled POELSTRAAT WOOD exceptionally heavily with Lac Shell. Prussic acid, Tear, Phosgene, chlorine Gas was used. Approx. 10,000 Gas Shells fell into the wood. Casualties: 3 Off. Lt. MURRAY (wounded gas) O.Ranks 18. (2 only gassed) Lt H CANTY (wounded shell shock) 2 Killed 15 wounded	

WAR DIARY
or
INTELLIGENCE SUMMARY
(Erase heading not required.)

Army Form C. 2118

June 1917

Place	Date	Hour	Summary of Events and Information	Remarks and references to Appendices
POLYGON WOOD	7/6/17	3.10 A.M	The 2nd ARMY attack on MESSINES RIDGE commenced. Heavy barrage put down by our guns. Enemy retaliated heavily with shells of all sizes. Mines blown by us. Shook the whole country side. No dugouts collapsed nor were any casualties caused by falling debris. 2 mines were blown in front of our left Company. Enemy's infantry was very active opposite us, but enemy M.G. fired continuously. All men of Our Battalion opened rapid fire in the front line for 15 minutes at 2.20 + 15 to 2.20 + 30. Casualties Officers: 20 wounded. 1 missing.	

WAR DIARY or INTELLIGENCE SUMMARY

Army Form C. 2118

Place	Date	Hour	Summary of Events and Information	Remarks and references to Appendices
PLOEGSTEERT WOOD	8/6/17	12 noon	Enemy continued to shell the whole sector with whizz bangs 4.5"5.9"	
			Our Artillery very active	
			Casualties. 15 O.R (wounded shell shock) 2nd/Lieut. W. INGHAM. 5 O.Ranks wounded	
	9/6/17		Artillery v. active on both sides	
			Casualties. 1 Off. LT. E.H. FARMER (wounded) 23 O.ranks wounded.	
	10/6/17		Artillery very active on both sides	
			Casualties. O.Ranks 2 wounded.	
	11/6/17	4.0 a.m	The Battalion was relieved by the 3rd Canterbury Battalion A.I.F. and marched over billets in ARMENTIERES	
			Casualties. O.Ranks 2 wounded	
ARMENTIERES	11/6/17		The Battalion marched to BAC ST MAUR & billeted	
BAC ST MAUR	12/6/17	10 pm	The Battalion was inspected by the G.O.C. 57th Division who expressed the men were complimented on their excellent work & devotion to duty during the intense bombardment which they were day & night subjected to, during the 8 days the Battalion held the Right flank of the 2nd ARMY attack. The Command of the 3rd Australian Division Col	

Army Form C. 2118

WAR DIARY
or
INTELLIGENCE SUMMARY
(Erase heading not required.)

June 1917.

Place	Date	Hour	Summary of Events and Information	Remarks and references to Appendices
R.H.Q. ST. MAUR	14/6/17	6.PM	The Battalion marched from R.H.Q. ST MAUR and billeted in the vicinity of ROUGE DEBOOT relieving the 1st West Riding Regt & taking over Bde Reserve of the CORDONNERIE SECTOR.	
CORDONNERIE SECTOR.	19/6/17	2.38P	The Battalion relieved the 7th L.N.L. in the CORDONNERIE SECTOR.	
	26/6/17	11.45P	The Battalion was relieved by the L.N.L. and took over Brigade Reserve.	
	30/6/17		Strength 32 Officers 756 Oranks.	

CONFIDENTIAL.

WAR DIARY.

OF

1/5 LOYAL NORTH LANCASHIRE REGT.

From July 1st 1917 To July 31st 1917.

VOLUME 6.

Army Form C. 2118

WAR DIARY
or
INTELLIGENCE SUMMARY
(Erase heading not required.)

July 1917. Vol. 6

Place	Date	Hour	Summary of Events and Information	Remarks and references to Appendices
CORDONNERIE SECTOR.	1/7/17.	12.0 am	Strength of Battalion 32 officers 756 o'ranks	
do	4/7/17	11.58 p	The Battalion relieved the 9th L.N.L. Regt taking over the Right Sub-sector	
do	13/9/17	11.30 p	The Battalion was relieved by the 9th Loyal N. Lanc. Regt	
do	20/7/17	11.0 p	The Battalion relieved the 9th L.N.Lanc. Regt	
do	27/7/17	11.30 pm	The Battalion carried out a Raid for the purpose of Killing and capturing the enemy for identification (Strength of Raiding Party 5 off. 98 o'ranks.) The Raiding party entered the enemy's Support Line & pushed forward a strong party to a road 150 yards further & lay up. Nothing was seen of the enemy at all. All arrangements & carrying out of the Raid went off perfectly. No Casualties.	BR Ent.
do	29/7/17	10.38 p	The above Raid was repeated with no success.	
do	31/7/17	7 pm	The Battalion moved from Billets at PONT DeBOUT to Billets in ARMENTIERES. Strength of Battalion 33 off. 803 o'ranks	
	31/7/17	min.		

CONFIDENTIAL.

WAR DIARY.

OF.

2/5 LOYAL NORTH LANCASHIRE REGT.

1917

FROM. August 1st 1917.   To. August 31st 1917.

Army Form C. 2118

WAR DIARY
or
INTELLIGENCE SUMMARY
(Erase heading not required.)

AUGUST 1917

Place	Date	Hour	Summary of Events and Information	Remarks and references to Appendices
ARMENTIERES	1/8/17	noon	Strength of Battalion. 32 officers 807 O.Ranks.	
L'Epinette Section	1/8/17	11.30 pm	The Battalion relieved 1/8 Bn (Irish) Kings (Liverpool Reg.) and took over the L'Epinette Section. I 6 a 28.67 to C 29 c 24.50.	
	6/8/17	10 pm	The enemy Gas Shelled the sector, a moderately dense concentration was effected. Casualties 3 O.Ranks.	
	10/8/17	8 pm	The enemy put down a heavy barrage on 'Left + Right Companies. This barrage outside about 8 to 15' commencing again at 9.0 pm with an intense bombardment lasting till 11.0 pm which concentrated on our Right Company which had been relieved during the day by the 1/4 Loyal N. Lancs. Regt. Our Casualties nil. The Battalion had 1 Officer (2nd Lt S. EASTWOOD) + 2 O.Ranks wounded.	
	10/8/17	12.05 am 11	The Battalion was relieved by the Loyal N. Lancs. Regt. + took over billets in Bde Reserve in ARMENTIERES.	
	20/8/17	11.30	The Battalion relieved the 4 Bn L.N. Lancs. Regt. The usual patrols were sent out, nothing unusual abnormal to report.	
	29/8/17	11.5 pm	The Battalion was relieved by 4 Bn Loyal N. Lancs. Regt took over billets in ARMENTIERES. 30 Officers 788 O.Ranks.	
	31/8/17			

CONFIDENTIAL.

WAR DIARY.
OF
2/5 Batt. LOYAL NORTH LANCASHIRE REGT.

Vol 8

From Sept. 1st 1917. To Sept. 30th 1917.

WAR DIARY or INTELLIGENCE SUMMARY

SEPTEMBER 1917

Army Form C. 2118.

Place	Date	Hour	Summary of Events and Information	Remarks and references to Appendices
ARMENTIERES	1/9/17	12 noon	Strength of Battalion 39 officers 789 O.R.'s	
	5/9/17	9.30 pm	The Battalion relieved in the F.R. north & south of the S'ganetti sector.	
	10/9/17	7.45-3 am	The enemy put over a large number of heavies on (R.o) producing a dense concentration about the support line. Roughly 900 Gas (Minnie.) shells were fired in this manner. Casualties 20 P. & E.R. Edgar 2/Lt Kilner. 7 O.R.'s all casualties were caused by the first which fortot amongst arnt. The "Minnie Gas shells were fired in salvoes of 10-15 at a time. During the remainder of the tour these were very annoying every day. Artillery fire normal.	
	13/9/17	10 pm	The Battalion was relieved by the 2nd Lancs Regt & 2 B.R. on the Reserve	
	15/9/17	11 pm	The Battalion was relieved by the 116 B.R. Sout. Wales Borderers and marched to "Waterlands Camp". R.20.a.2.6. (sheet 36.2.6. Regt.France). & billeted	
	18/9/17	9 am	The Battalion marched from WATERLANDS CAMP to LA GORGUE where it billets for the night	
	19/9/17	6.30 am	The Battalion marched from LA GORGUE to CANTRAINNE & billets for the night	

Army Form C. 2118.

WAR DIARY
or
INTELLIGENCE SUMMARY.

(Erase heading not required.)

September 1917

Instructions regarding War Diaries and Intelligence Summaries are contained in F.S. Regs., Part II and the Staff Manual respectively. Title pages will be prepared in manuscript.

Place	Date	Hour	Summary of Events and Information	Remarks and references to Appendices
CANTRAINE	20/9/17	8.30am	The Battalion marched from BIEFS ox CANTRAINE to WESTREHEM where Billets were taken over preparatory to commencing Training	
	24/9/17	9am	The Battalion commenced Training	
	25/9/17	8pm	Reinforcement draft arrived 129 O.Ranks. 1 officer 2/Lt J.N. BOYLE	
	27/9/17	"	" 2 officers 2nd Lt W. MALTON 2nd Lt L.F. GUY.	
	29/9/17	1pm	One officer reported for duty 2nd Lt M.J. MIDDLEHURST.	
	30/9/17	noon	Strength of Battalion 38 officers 895 O.Ranks.	

CONFIDENTIAL

Vol 9

WAR DIARY
OF
2/5 Bn. LOYAL NORTH LANCASHIRE REGT.

From October 1st 1917. to October 31st 1917.

Army Form C. 2118.

WAR DIARY
or
INTELLIGENCE SUMMARY.
(Erase heading not required)

OCTOBER 1917

Place	Date	Hour	Summary of Events and Information	Remarks and references to Appendices
WESTREHEM	11/10/17	9 am	Strength of Battalion 38 off 895 O.Ranks. (No change) The Battalion took part in a Brigade exercise in the Manoeuvre Area near BOMY.	
	2nd 3rd		Training	
	4th 5th		–do–	
	6/10/17		The Battalion was inspected by Lt. Gen. Maxwell Emery in Chief Eastern Army. Marsh	
	7/10/17 Sat		The Battalion took part in Brigade Operations (Training)	
	17th		–do–	
	19th	9 am	The Battalion left WESTREHEM by march route to RENESCURE billets	
LONGUE-CONE	18th	10 a.m.	– RENESCURE by Bus to PROVEN. AREA Nº 2 Encampment	
PROVEN-CAMP	22nd	11.30 am	The Battalion left PROVEN Area Nº 2 by tram to BOESINGHE	
NR 4TH DIV. FM			thence detrained & marched to MARSOUIN FM Camp & there bivouacked for the night	
Bus N.E.	24th	5pm	The Battalion left MARSOUIN FM Camp & moved to the line enfilading Companies & taxied in the line relieving the 20th Northumberland Fusiliers	
WIELTJE			Frontage of Battalion from V.14.C.6.8 to V.14.a.00.95. Bn.H.Q. SCHAPPAERE H.11.m	

WAR DIARY
or
INTELLIGENCE SUMMARY.

Army Form C. 2118.

OCTOBER 1917

Place	Date	Hour	Summary of Events and Information	Remarks and references to Appendices
Trs: M.G. BIEFVILLERS	25th	5.00pm	The Battalion completed its relief by 23rd Yorkshires during the evening. Only 2 casualties during relief, the carried out through heavy shelling. In the afternoon the line when the front anomalies of our front was enemy shelled heavily at intervals & the Battalion had 53 Casualties Others.	
	26th	3.40am	The Battalion formed up for the attack in an Artillery 100yds from our original line. The forming up on the tape line was carried out very well & without many casualties as the ground & weather conditions were exceedingly bad.	
		5.20am	The Battn advanced to the attack in 4 500 yds front with platoons & coys in "Artillery" attack formation. 3 Coys in the front line & 1 as Support Coy. Each Platoon having a frontage of about 100yds. The going was almost impossible due to the state of the ground, however the men moved forward steadily	CW

WAR DIARY or INTELLIGENCE SUMMARY

Army Form C. 2118.

1917 OCTOBER

Place	Date	Hour	Summary of Events and Information	Remarks and references to Appendices
[Passchendaele]			Early the enemy were seen to run and troops before day came under of intense M.G. fire, which caused a great number of casualties. The B.L. position had been moved by our troops. All Coy officers of the B. became casualties during the early stages of the attack, but the N.C.O's + Privates carried on the advance in a most determined manner. It is estimated that our casualties were 500 of men wounded + killed. Still less than 700 to 800 of somewhat doing very arduous fighting. It was not known till late that was fought that the very thin line had been driven back to our original position + everything lost. The enemy seemed to anticipate the attack + prepared themselves and great numbers of men lay close to our line, when even + taking these troops moved our barrage + entered our entry lines.	9

WAR DIARY
INTELLIGENCE SUMMARY

Army Form C. 2118.

OCTOBER 9

Place	Date	Hour	Summary of Events and Information	Remarks and references to Appendices
W.F.				

During heavy continuous rain initial stages of the attack.

The Enemy Snipers were very efficient, it is most important that all ranks are sniper alike as anybody advancing covered (ie by forcing Snipers or cheating are annihilated. Sniped.

The heavy casualties were mostly due to M.G. fire. The ground which had to be advanced over was dreadful. It speaks well of/for men that they got down at all & were almost unhampered.

Enemy M.G. were mostly beaten in stretchers, all M.Gs bringing across fire from one or the other flanks. It was found almost impossible to take the clip to the mud which collects on the rifle when swimming. Yet it nearly) the area waist deep in water.

WAR DIARY or INTELLIGENCE SUMMARY

Army Form C. 2118.

OCTOBER 9 (1917)

Place	Date	Hour	Summary of Events and Information	Remarks and references to Appendices

As it was almost impossible to find a Lt. to take the Bayonet and all the officers being wounded of which the men of the Battalion received information. The leading feature of the attack was the fact that N.C.O. so splendidly led their men in & often an Officer became casualty early on & the advance it is stated that within half an hour of the attack 500 Germans + 2 German M.G. Coy Snipers caused & no further killed & German M.G. Coy Snipers caused & no further advance when to become a casualty. Personal messages. Casualties: 6 officers killed, 6 officers wounded, Officers wounded Capt H Cleaver 2nd Lt. A.T. Marshall

H.B. Parks killed

Officers killed: Capt A.S. Hake.
Capt N. Morris
Lieut. R. Grey.
2nd Lt. J.C. Hartley
2nd Lt. T. Middlehurst

L. T. Ryans 2nd Lt. Neil Brown
10. Ambulance Lieut. H. Drysdale
2nd Lt. Enwright.
2nd Lt. H. Paton
2nd Lt. W. Halton

WAR DIARY
or
INTELLIGENCE SUMMARY.

(Erase heading not required.)

Army Form C. 2118.

OCTOBER 9 1917

Place	Date	Hour	Summary of Events and Information	Remarks and references to Appendices
In the field	26/9	3.0 a.m.	The Battalion was relieved by the 2/8 K. Kings Shrop Light Inf &	
HUDDLESTON(?)	27/9 Mon		moved to HUDDLESTON CAMP	
		9.30	The Battalion marched to BOESINGHE & entrained at PROVEN	
		12.30	— hauled from PROVEN STATION to PEPPINGTON	
			camp where it encamped.	
	28/9		The Battalion was taken the equipped & clothes	
	29/9		The Battalion was re-organised	
	30/9	7 a.m.	Strength of Battalion — 23 off. 615 Oranks. (Total strength)	

CONFIDENTIAL.

WAR DIARY.
OF.
2/5 BATTALION LOYAL NORTH LANCS. REGT.

From November 1st 1917.
To November 30th 1917.

Vn 10   10.

Army Form C. 2118.

WAR DIARY
or
INTELLIGENCE SUMMARY.
(Erase heading not required.)

NOVEMBER 1917

Instructions regarding War Diaries and Intelligence
Summaries are contained in F. S. Regs., Part II.
and the Staff Manual respectively. Title pages
will be prepared in manuscript.

Place	Date	Hour	Summary of Events and Information	Remarks and references to Appendices
PROVEN.	1/11/17	12 Noon	Strength of the Battalion 27 Officers 594 O. Ranks.	
AREA No 1.	2/11/17		Re-equipping of the Battalion.	
REDDINGTON CAMP	3/11/17	11.00 a.m	My Battalion was inspected at Training by the Army Commander General Sir H de la P Gough KCB KCVO	
	8/11/17	6 a.m	The Battalion moved from PROVEN by Train to AUDRUICQ. T marches from AUDRUICQ Station to AUDENFORT Area Billets	
AUDENFORT	10/11/17		The Battalion commenced Training continued 10/11/17 to 30/11/17.	
	30/11/17	12 Noon	Strength of Battalion, 30 officers 664 O. Ranks.	

CONFIDENTIAL.

WAR DIARY

OF

2/5 Bn. LOYAL NORTH LANCS. REGT.

From Dec 1st 1917. To Dec 31st 1917.

WAR DIARY
or
INTELLIGENCE SUMMARY.

(Erase heading not required.)

Army Form C. 2118.

DECEMBER 1917

Place	Date	Hour	Summary of Events and Information	Remarks and references to Appendices
AUDENFORT	1/12/17	12.0m.	Strength of Battalion. 31 Officers 693 Oranks.	
	11/12/17	10.0am	The Battalion entrained at AUDENFORT and moved to PROVEN where debussed and encamped at PENTON CAMP. (CANADA HUTS) PROVEN	
	13/12/17	8.45a.	The Battalion moved from PENTON CAMP to CLAUDE CAMP (ROUSBRUGGE - MR. N.4.H.2) by march route	
	16/12/17	8.10a.	The Battalion marched from ROUSBRUGGE-HARINGHE to DYKES CAMP DE-WIPPE AREA (ELVERDINGHE) and took over as Pt Bn. Brigade Rifle Service. The Battalion furnished working parties to the forward area.	
	19/4/17 to		do	Casualties - NIL.
	29/12/19		do	
	30/12/17	3.0a.	The Battalion was relieved by A Bn SPN 55 Infble and marched to PORTSMOUTH CAMP. PEOSSDY AREA PROVEN and encamped.	
	31/12/17	12 nn	Strength of Battalion 40 officers 667 oranks.	

WAR DIARY
or
INTELLIGENCE SUMMARY.
(Erase heading not required.)

Army Form C. 2118.

JANUARY 1918

12

Place	Date	Hour	Summary of Events and Information	Remarks and references to Appendices
PORTSMOUTH CAMP PROVEN	1/1/18	p.m.	Strength of Battalion 39 Officers 668 O.Ranks.	
	2/1/18	7 a.m.	The Battalion left PORTSMOUTH CAMP. PROVEN, entrained at PROVEN STA. 9 a.m. & moved by Rail to BAILLEUL a/one detrained & marched to & encamped at MOULLE BAIX CAMP STEENWERCK AREA.	
WIZMACQUART SECTOR.	8/1/19	9 a.m.	The Battalion moved into the Line and relieved the 44th Australian Bn. (11 Aust Bde 3rd Div.) in Close Support of the WIZMACQUART SECTOR. 3 Coys in Close Support & 1 Coy & S.A.S.A. Coy HQrs Ybarre Switch.	
WIZMACQUART SECTOR.	14/1/18 to 15/1/18		The Coy of this Bn. garrisoning PACORIA SWITCH carried out intensive work in improving the defences of the same. The other 3 Coys worked under instruction of the Bn. Commander holding the Front Line Eye Rows.	
do.	15/1/18	10-20 p.m.	The Bn. was relieved by the 7/8 R.K.O.R. Regt. and moved to trench — equipment as Bn. in Reserve.	
do.	20/1/19	5.30	The Bn. relieved the 7/8 Kings Own 24 Regt. Close Support and carried out work in improving defences.	

Army Form C. 2118.

WAR DIARY
or
INTELLIGENCE SUMMARY.

(Erase heading not required.)

JANUARY 1918

12

Instructions regarding War Diaries and Intelligence Summaries are contained in F. S. Regs., Part II. and the Staff Manual respectively. Title pages will be prepared in manuscript.

Place	Date	Hour	Summary of Events and Information	Remarks and references to Appendices
WEZ MACQUART	25/1/18	5.30 p.m	The Bn. was relieved by 9/5th KO R L Regt. and occupied Reserve position in ERQUINGHEM as Bn. in Brigade Reserve.	
	26/1/18	5.0.	The Bn. relieved the 9/5th Kings Own R.L. Regt in Close Support and carried on work in the afternoon.	
	29/1/18	5.30 p.m	The Bn. was relieved by The Kings Own R.L. Regt. and occupied positions in ERQUINGHEM as Battalion in Brigade Reserve.	
	31/1/18	11 a.m	Strength of Bn. 39 Officers 646 Oraks.	

57TH DIVISION
170TH INFY BDE

4-5TH BN LOY. NTH LANCS

~~FEB 1917 — JAN 1918~~

1915 OCT — 1916 FEB
1917 FEB — 1918 JAN

~~DISBANDED~~

AMALGAMATED WITH 1/5 BN.

www.ingramcontent.com/pod-product-compliance
Lightning Source LLC
Chambersburg PA
CBHW081459160426
43193CB00013B/2537